DATE DUE

NOV 24 '87			
APR 22 '88			
MAY 20 '88			
JUN 3 '88			
JUN 2 8 1991			
JUN 2 8 1991			
NOV 3 0 1991			
NOV 3 0 1991			
FEB 27			
OCT 17			

3/20/85

ENERGY FROM FOSSIL FUELS

To my children Brandon and Kristin,
whose future depends on energy

Library of Congress Number: 82-9805

1234567890   8786858483

Library of Congress Cataloging in Publication Data

Rice, Dale.
  Energy from fossil fuels.

  (A Look inside)
  Includes index.
  SUMMARY: Describes the origins of coal, natural gas,
and petroleum, explaining how they are refined and used
to produce energy.
  1. Power resources — Juvenile literature. 2. Fossil
fuels — Juvenile literature. [1. Fossil fuels.
2. Power resources] I. Title. II. Series.
TJ163.23.R5 1982   553.2   82-9805
ISBN 0-8172-1417-8   AACR2

ENERGY FROM FOSSIL FUELS

By Dale Rice

CONTENTS

RAINTREE PUBLISHERS
Milwaukee • Toronto • Mexico City • London

553.2

HOW FOSSIL FUELS ARE FORMED

Publishers Telemarketing

Millions of years ago, the climate on earth was much different from what it is today. Large parts of the earth were hot and swampy. Other parts were covered by ancient seas. Tiny animals lived in the seas. Huge, strange plants grew in the swamps. Scientists know how these plants and animals looked, because impressions of the plants and animals were preserved as fossils. A fossil was formed when an imprint of the plant or animal was made in the mud of the swamp or sea bottom. When the mud hardened into rock, the imprint was preserved.

The plants and animals in the swamp grew up, died, and fell to the ground. When the plants and animals in the sea died, they settled to the sea floor. This went on for thousands of years. Eventually a thick layer of dead plants and animals covered the ground and sea floor.

Over thousands of years, small rocks and layers of sediments covered the dead plants and ani-

This painting shows animals of the Pliocene Age drinking at a lake.

mals. (Sediments are mud, sand, or gravel.) The layers of sediment turned into "sedimentary" rocks. Sedimentary rocks are formed when layers of small rocks and minerals come together to form one large rock. Shale, limestone, and sandstone are examples of sedimentary rocks.

Pressure and decay made the dead animals and plants in the rocks change into fossil fuels: coal, oil, and natural gas. These fossil fuels collected in and around the sedimentary rocks.

Some people say that fossil fuels are stored sunshine. Plants use the energy from sunshine, along with water, and carbon dioxide from the air, to make food. When an animal eats a plant, it eats the plant's stored energy. And when that plant or animal dies, the energy becomes a part of the earth's crust. Fossil fuels are really stored energy from the sun; energy which reached the earth millions of years ago.

This prehistoric scene shows a cross section of the earth as well as plants and animals that were then living on the earth. Within these layers of rock, dead plants and animals have already begun to change to fossil fuels.

COAL

The coal found on earth began forming 350 million years ago. Scientists call this period in the history of the earth the Carboniferous period, or the Coal Age. Coal was formed when the process of plant and animal decay slowed down. Water, oxygen, and nitrogen gases from plant and animal remains were released into the air. The carbon from the remains stayed trapped under the sediments and water, and formed a jellylike mass. More layers of sediment added pressure to the buried plants and animals. This pressure compacted, or squeezed together, the jellylike mass.

The burial and compaction turned the mass into a carbon-rich material. More sediment built up and squeezed the material. The compacted carbon eventually formed a coal bed.

Coal beds range from a fraction of a centimeter to several meters thick. Some coal beds are near the surface. Others are deep within the earth. The reason for this is that the surface of the earth has changed. Over many centuries new mountains have grown and been worn away. Valleys and plains have also formed and changed. Some coal beds have been brought to the surface. Others have been buried deep.

Peat is the first step in the formation of coal. Peat is a brownish black, spongy substance which looks like decayed wood. It can be found near the surface of the earth in bogs and swamps. It contains some carbon and can be burned. When burned, it gives off a lot of smoke, but little heat and energy.

Compaction turns peat into other forms of coal. During the second step in coal formation, lignite coal is formed. Like peat, lignite is brownish black, but it has more carbon in it.

Additional pressure and compaction turns lignite into bituminous coal. It takes about ten meters (33 ft) of peat to make thirty centimeters (1 ft) of bituminous coal. Bituminous coal is sometimes called soft coal. It's about half carbon. Some types of bituminous coal which contain less carbon are called sub-bituminous coal. Sub-bituminous coal is very soft. It can be used for heat and energy in factories.

Bituminous coal is the most common type of coal found on earth. It is used to produce most of the electricity used in the United States.

Further compaction and pressure produce anthracite coal. Anthracite coal is about 95 percent carbon. It is sometimes called hard coal. Anthracite coal is very rare. It can be found in only a few places on the earth, such as the eastern parts of Pennsylvania. It is hard to burn, so it is not usually used for electricity.

Coal can be found in North

In one operation, this continous miner removes coal from a mine wall and then loads the coal into a shuttle car, which takes the coal to the surface.

National Coal Association

America, the USSR, China, South Africa, India, and Australia. However, most of the coal in the world can be found in North America. Canada and the United States have almost half of all the coal found in the world.

Even though we have so much coal, we do not use it as much as other fossil fuels. When it is burned, it can form a poisonous gas called sulfur dioxide. This can get into the air, along with ash from the burned coal. It is difficult and expensive to stop this air pollution. It is also quite dangerous to mine coal. However, we have so much coal that we will probably use more of it in the future.

OIL

In some sedimentary rocks, the decaying plants and animals changed into small oil droplets. Like water which seeps into a sponge, the oil droplets seeped into the small openings in the sedimentary rocks. This process continued for thousands of years.

Eventually the oil droplets reached rocks that they could not pass through. These rocks are called impermeable rocks. An impermeable rock is a rock which does not have small openings between the rock pieces. The impermeable rocks acted like a cap on top of the sedimentary rocks. The oil droplets were trapped, and large oil pools formed. The oil pools contained crude oil, which is also called petroleum.

Crude oil is about 82 percent carbon and 15 percent hydrogen. Oxygen and nitrogen make up the other 3 percent. Crude oil is sometimes called a hydrocarbon. It gets its name from the main elements found in it, hydrogen and carbon.

Oil pools can be found where the ancient seas once covered the land. They can also be found in the shallow waters off the coasts of many countries. The greatest supply of crude oil is in the Middle East. Kuwait, Iran, Arabia and Iraq produce most of the

An onshore drilling rig.

world's crude oil. In the United States, crude oil has been found in many southwestern states and in the Gulf of Mexico. The largest deposit of crude oil in the United States has been found in Prudhoe Bay on the frozen north coast of Alaska.

NATURAL GAS

Natural gas is formed in much the same way as crude oil. Decaying plants and animals trapped in sedimentary rocks formed oil droplets. Some oil droplets received particularly strong heat and pressure. This squeezed gas out of the oil. Most of the oil changed completely into natural gas.

The gas made its way upward through the sedimentary rocks. Sometimes the gas reached the surface and escaped into the air.

Natural gas is kept in tanks like these at a gas separation plant.

the oil droplets have already changed to natural gas. However, when all the oil droplets have not changed, natural gas can be found at the top of an oil pool, or mixed in with the oil.

Natural gas is a hydrocarbon like oil and coal. It is mostly made up of a colorless, odorless gas called methane. Gas companies add a chemical to natural gas to give it an odor. The odor makes it possible to smell natural gas. In this way, leaks in gas pipelines can be found and fixed.

Large deposits of natural gas are found in many areas of the world, such as the Soviet Union and Iran. In the United States, most of the natural gas can be found in six states: Texas, Louisiana, Alaska, New Mexico, Kansas and Oklahoma. These six states produce nearly 90 percent of all the natural gas used in the United States in a year. Long-distance pipelines carry the natural gas to other states.

The Trans-Alaskan Pipeline (right) carries oil some 1300 kilometers (800 mi) from the northern coast to the southern coast of Alaska.

You can see this in swampy areas today, where bubbles of gas rise up through the water. Like the oil droplets, the rest of the natural gas was trapped by impermeable rocks.

Over millions of years, huge amounts of gas collected. Most natural gas deposits are not found near oil pools, because all

THE DISCOVERY OF FOSSIL FUELS

Fossil fuels have been used by people of all countries for thousands of years. An early Italian explorer, Marco Polo, visited China in 1275 and wrote that the Chinese used coal to heat iron and copper. The Romans and Greeks also used coal to heat their forges and homes. In fact, the Bible mentions the use of coal in the Book of Proverbs (26:21).

The use of coal became widespread in England during the beginning of the Industrial Revolution, in the late eighteenth century. The steam engine developed by James Watt made it possible to power many factories. These plants had depended on wind or water power before. Now, more coal needed to be mined. The coal industry was started to help find and mine the coal needed.

Coal was first used in America by the Native Americans. They used coal for making clay jars and vases. In 1750, a young boy living near what is now Richmond, Virginia discovered a huge coal bed. Soon afterward the first commercial coal mine opened there.

However, coal was not widely used in America until the middle 1800s. Railroads needed large amounts of coal to run the giant steam engine locomotives. Steam engines were also being used in electrical generating plants. The coal was burned to heat water. That made steam which turned blades in an electrical generator. The first power station in America to use coal was the Pearl Street Power Station. It started producing electricity in New York City on September 4, 1882.

Many changes in producing electricity have occurred during the last 100 years. But coal is still being used to run electrical generators. Over half of the electricity now produced in the United States is fueled by coal.

Another use of coal is to make steel. To make steel, coal is converted to coke. This is done by baking coal in large, air-tight ovens. The coke is then mixed with iron ore in very hot blast furnaces. The coke melts and cleans out unwanted minerals from the iron ore. Molten (liquid) iron is formed. The iron is used to make steel. Certain chemicals, cement, and textiles are also made from coal.

Coal is the most common fossil fuel. However, oil and natural gas are used more to produce energy. Nearly 75 percent of all the energy produced in the United States — electricity, heating, gasoline for cars — comes from oil and natural gas.

Oil, like coal, has been used for thousands of years. Ancient boatmen used a form of oil to cover their reed boats. Asphalt, another form of oil, was also used to pave roads in some ancient cities. The early Native Americans of North America used oil for fuel and medicine. In the mid-1800s some oil found seeping up to the earth's surface was used to make kerosene. The kerosene was used for lighting lamps.

On August 27, 1859, oil was

The photograph above shows the Drake Well—the world's first successful oil well. It was about a half-mile from Titusville, Pennsylvania. Drilling was completed on August 27, 1859, by Edwin L. Drake (inset). The Drake Well marked the birth of the petroleum industry.

The other old-time well (left) was about 365 meters (1200 ft) deep.

struck on a farm near Titusville, Pennsylvania. Edwin Drake had built an oil well to drill for oil for the Pennsylvania Rock Oil Company. Drake struck oil at a depth of 21 meters (70 ft). Soon an oil boom started around Titusville and Pennsylvania. In the next few years thousands of oil wells were drilled. The crude oil from these early wells was refined to make kerosene. To "refine" something is to make it pure, and clean out unwanted materials.

In the early 1900s automobiles were becoming common. They needed gasoline to run, so crude oil was refined to make gasoline. To supply the millions of cars on the road today, over half of all crude oil is used for gasoline.

Refined crude oil can be used for many products other than gasoline. Heating oil, jet fuels, and asphalt are made from crude oil. Oil is also used to make plastic, fertilizers, and detergents. Almost everything we use depends in some way on oil and oil products.

Scientists have found evidence that natural gas was used by ancient people. Thousands of years ago the Chinese discovered a way to get salt, using natural gas. Natural gas was piped to containers of salt water through bamboo poles. There it was burned, and the salt water evaporated. Salt was left behind.

The first gas company was formed in 1812 in England. In 1821, William Hart built the first natural gas well in America, near Fredonia, New York. The gas from the well was used to light nearby buildings. Other cities began using natural gas for lighting during the mid-1800s.

When oil was discovered, few people remained interested in natural gas. In some cases, people became upset if they found natural gas when they were drilling for oil. They would usually just release the gas into the air. Little use could be found for the gas except for lighting. Natural gas burns very easily, and explosions and fires were frequent. It was very dangerous to send from one place to another. Then new pipes were invented that could safely carry natural gas. Today hundreds of kilometers of pipelines take natural gas everywhere in the United States.

Natural gas is used to heat homes and industries. It is also used to make plastics, explosives, film, dishes, fertilizers, and paints, among other things.

An early touring car.

SEARCHING FOR FOSSIL FUELS

A scientist who studies the structure and history of the earth is called a geologist. A geologist knows that sedimentary rocks may contain oil and natural gas. Other kinds of rocks may show where coal beds can be found. Using complicated scientific instruments and tools, a geologist looks for fossil fuels. They are not easy to find. Coal, oil and natural gas are sometimes buried under hundreds of meters of rock.

Geologists have several ways to find out what is hidden below the earth's surface. For instance, they can set off a small underground explosion with dynamite. Shock waves from the explosion travel through the rocks under the earth's surface. An instrument called a seismograph records the shock waves as they bounce off the layers of rocks. It draws a special picture of the waves. Geologists study this. Then they decide if fossil fuels may be found in the sedimentary rocks.

Another way geologists figure

This isometric map was created by a computer. The map shows geologic structure deep in the earth.

out what is hidden under the surface is by an instrument called a magnetometer. A magnetometer can record differences in the earth's magnetism. Certain rocks which contain oil or natural gas have a difference in their magnetism. When large differences occur in the instrument's readings, oil and natural gas may lie underground.

A third tool geologists use is a gravimeter. A gravimeter records differences in the earth's gravity. Each rock has a certain density. Density is how close the parts of a rock fit together. Some rocks are more dense than others. Rocks whose density is less than the rocks around them have less gravitational pull. These rocks may hold oil and natural gas.

One of a geophysicist's jobs is to interpret information about an area in order to determine whether there could be oil, coal, or natural gas beneath the surface.

If an area looks promising, a core sample may be taken. A core sample is made by drilling down into the earth. Then the geologist pulls a long section out of the ground. He or she examines the different layers of rocks in the core sample. If all the tests look promising, the area may be mined for coal, or drilled for oil and natural gas.

These scientists are aboard a ship studying geophysical data. Some fossil fuels are found in the earth beneath bodies of water.

MINING FOR COAL

The earth has undergone many changes over the last 350 million years. Some of the coal which was formed millions of years ago is near the earth's surface. Other deposits of coal can be found hundreds of meters underground. Before people can use coal, it must be recovered.

There are two ways to recover the earth's coal: surface mining and underground mining. Surface mining is called strip mining. Underground mining involves three methods. These methods are slope, drift and shaft mining.

A huge earth-moving machine rolling across former farmlands or forests is a familiar sight to many people in coal-producing states. The machines can be more than 50 stories high. One bite from the huge shovels can remove more than 325 tons of material from the earth's surface. Over 3500 tons of rocks and dirt can be dug out in one hour. This rock and dirt is called overburden. The shovels dig out the overburden until they reach the coal bed. Miners then break the coal up with explosives. Smaller shovels load the coal into trucks. The trucks carry the coal to processing plants.

As more coal is needed to produce energy, more strip mining may take place in the future. It is a safer and easier method of mining than underground mining. Less equipment and fewer special procedures are needed. It is also less expensive.

Unfortunately, huge pits are created in areas that have been strip mined. Valuable farmlands and forests may have been destroyed. Recently, laws have been

A strip mine in Black Mesa, Arizona.

passed which require strip mine owners to restore the land to its former condition. These laws have helped stop the ugly destruction. Parks and lakes have been created where strip mines once were. Farmers now grow crops and raise cattle in some areas. In other places young forests now flourish.

Sometimes coal lies too far below the surface to be reached by strip mining. Then underground mining is used to reach the coal. Most of the coal in the United States comes from underground mining.

If a coal bed is not too deep, a

Lake Hope—in Lake Hope State Park, Ohio—is a reclaimed coal strip mine.

This is a flexible roof drill. It removes coal from the roof of a mine tunnel.

slope mine is used. A long, slowly slanting tunnel is dug into the earth. Miners reach the coal by walking down the slope. In some cases small electric cars carry the miners to the coal bed. Coal is brought to the surface in small cars, or on a long conveyer belt.

Coal which is found on the side of a hill is reached by a drift mine. The entrance to the mine is on the side of the hill where the coal bed starts. The miners tunnel into the hill, removing the coal as they go. As in the slope mine, coal is removed by small electric cars or a long conveyer belt.

Shaft mining is used when coal beds lie far below the earth's surface. A long tunnel is dug straight down into the earth until it reaches the coal bed. The tunnel is widened until it is large enough to carry miners and machines by elevator to the coal bed. More tunnels are made away from the shaft. These tunnels follow the coal beds. Miners use special equipment to take the coal to the surface.

Miners must be very careful. The air in the mine must be tested. Coal dust, which can explode, is controlled by spraying powdered limestone in work areas. Cave-ins are stopped by placing steel rods in the mine ceiling. Still, coal mining is very dangerous. Coal dust can cause a disease called black lung. Some cave-ins and explosions can still occur. New laws have been passed to make coal mining safer.

This is a close-up view of an auger bit. It drills a hole into the wall of a mine and removes the coal.

DRILLING FOR OIL AND NATURAL GAS

Offshore oil-drilling equipment.

Drilling for oil and natural gas has changed greatly since Edwin Drake first drilled for oil in 1859. Today complicated equipment and highly trained people are used to drill for oil and natural gas.

Once the scientists have found a spot which may contain oil or natural gas, a derrick is built. The derrick is a large steel structure. It can be 25 to 60 meters (80 to 200 ft) tall. The derrick is used to put together the drill pipe and to lift it in and out of the hole being drilled.

Several methods are used to drill for oil. The most common method is called rotary drilling. In rotary drilling a large drill bit bores into the earth. The drill bit has big, gearlike teeth which turn around and around to tear apart the rocks under the earth's surface. The teeth of the drill bit are made from very hard steel and diamonds.

When the rotating drill bit reaches a depth of nine meters it stops. The derrick crew adds a new section of drill pipe. Then the drilling starts again. The drilling stops every nine meters so that another drill pipe section can be added. The drilled hole may go down into the earth for more than 3000 meters. Drilling for oil and natural gas goes on day and night for many days.

Water containing clay and chemicals, called the drilling mud, is spread over the drill bit. Pieces of rock being drilled stick to the mud and are brought to the surface. Drilling mud brought back to the surface is cleared of the rock pieces and used again. The drill hole is enclosed in a steel pipe. This prevents the oil or natural gas from escaping into other layers of rock.

Scientists study very carefully the rocks being brought to the surface. The derrick crew also watches the drilling process. When oil or natural gas is reached they want to prevent a gusher. A gusher is when oil and natural gas under pressure rush to the surface. To prevent a gusher, a device with many valves and pipes, called a "Christmas Tree," is added to the top of the well. The valves work like the faucets on sinks. They can stop or start the flow of oil or natural gas. From the Christmas Tree, oil and natural gas flow into other pipes to be sent to refineries or pumping stations.

Only one well drilled in ten ever finds oil or natural gas. In some cases, when oil and natural gas is found it must be pumped out of the well. Sometimes water is forced into the well to bring it to the surface. The equipment is very complicated and must be run by highly skilled professionals. Drilling for oil and natural gas is very expensive.

This photograph was taken in about 1900. It shows an oil gusher at the Lucas oil well.

FOSSIL FUELS IN THE FUTURE

For over 100 years coal, oil and natural gas have provided energy for people living on the earth. This energy has enabled the people of the earth to let machines do more and more of their work. It has helped make people's lives more comfortable. New products have been developed using the energy from fossil fuels.

The people of the earth are very dependent on the energy from fossil fuels. Every day brings more demands for more energy. The amount of energy used each year in the United States has increased about eight times in this century. People in the United States use about one-fourth of all energy produced on earth. This is a huge amount compared to other countries in the world.

The tremendous use of energy has placed a big demand on finding new deposits of fossil fuels. Geologists and other scientists have been improving their methods of locating fossil fuels. With more research, ways may be found to increase the amount of oil and natural gas taken from wells. Satellites and new computer technology will help us find new deposits of fossil fuels.

Offshore drilling for oil and natural gas produces almost 25 percent of the oil and natural gas used in the United States. Most offshore drilling rigs are now located off the coasts of Alaska and California. Others can be found in the Gulf of Mexico. Recently, experts have predicted that more large stores of oil and natural gas may be found on sites not now being used. Scientists have found three areas off the east coast of the U.S. which probably contain oil and natural gas.

Many people are against offshore drilling. Offshore drilling could cause the pollution of coastal waters. A serious oil spill at Santa Barbara, California destroyed many coastal plants and animals. Offshore drilling is also five times more expensive than drilling for oil and natural gas on land.

Even if offshore drilling can be made safe and all additional deposits found, more energy will still be needed. Scientists are now working on experimental methods of providing energy.

Stockphotos, Inc.

Both of these pictures show offshore oil-drilling rigs. The one on the right has a cantilever jackup.

One method which may be used in the future is to use coal to produce gas. This process is called coal gasification. Some experimental plants are now using coal to produce natural gas. Coal supplies make up 75 percent of all fossil fuel reserves in the United States. Natural gas forms no pollution when burned. Turning coal to natural gas will eliminate the problems of air pollution now caused by burning coal. Coal gasification will be one method used to increase energy production in the future.

This chemist (left) is looking at a jar filled with gasoline that was made from coal. In his left hand is a jar of heavy oil that was also made from coal.

American Petroleum Institute

In some areas of the world huge deposits of tar sands can be found. Tar sands may be used in the future to produce oil. The oil in tar sands does not flow. It looks like a very thick tar or asphalt. The oil in tar sands cannot be obtained by drilling a well, because it is so thick. It can be taken out of the sand in two ways. One way involves heating up the rocks and sand. This makes the asphalt melt. Oil can then be taken from the asphalt.

The other way is to mine the tar sands. Rocks containing the

This is what tar sand looks like before (right) and after (left) the oil has been scrubbed out.

thick asphalt deposits can be reached through strip mining or underground mining. Mining tar sands is similar to mining coal. The mined rocks in the tar sand deposit are heated in special containers. Once heated, the asphalt in the rocks begins to melt. The flowing asphalt is processed to produce oil. The largest deposit of tar sands is in Alberta, Canada. Energy is being produced on a large scale from these tar sands. In the future other deposits and methods of mining tar sands may be found.

Oil shale is another possible future way to get oil and natural gas. Shale is a sedimentary rock which contains small deposits of oil. To get the oil, the shale is heated and the vapor released is cooled. When the vapor cools, it turns into a liquid. The liquid is oil. Oil from oil shales is not being used right now. It is still too expensive and difficult to produce. As more energy is needed in the future, oil shales may become an important energy source.

People have been using fossil fuels faster than new reserves have been found. The new developments used in obtaining fossil fuels, such as offshore drilling, coal gasification, tar sands, and oil shales will not provide enough energy for the future. Until future energy sources are developed, people will have to conserve energy.

The conservation of energy is easy to do. Lights should be turned off when not in use. Air conditioners should be set at higher temperatures during the summer. During the winter the thermostat should be set at lower temperatures. People should learn to use car pools, or public transportation. Buildings should be well insulated.

It is important that everyone conserves energy. In this way, energy resources will be available to all the people of the earth.

The photo at the right shows the gasification of coal in the tumbling bed of a rotary ported kiln.

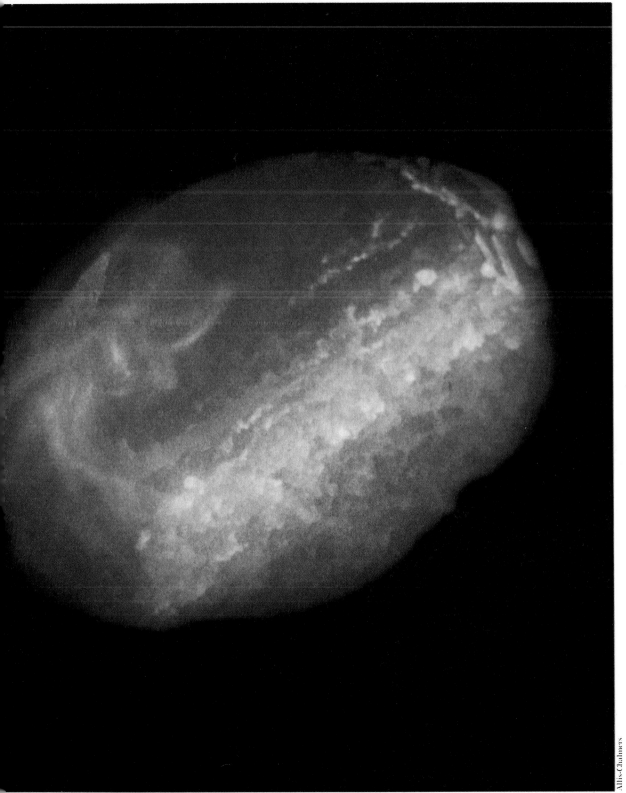

ENERGY SOURCES OF THE FUTURE

A solar oven.

It takes millions of years for fossil fuels to form. However, at the current rate of use, all of the oil and natural gas in the world will be gone by the year 2080. Coal is much more plentiful and will last another 300 years. Soon the earth will run out of energy unless new ways to produce energy are found.

Some possible energy sources in the future are solar energy, nuclear energy, tidal energy, wind energy and geothermal energy.

Solar energy uses energy directly from the sun. A large solar collector collects the sun's heat. The heat warms buildings and heats water. Energy from the sun is very common and easy to use. All that is needed is a solar collector. Unfortunately, only certain areas of the world get enough sunshine to use solar energy. Solar energy cannot be collected at night. Also, it can be very costly to build houses that are powered by solar collectors.

Nuclear energy could provide an almost unlimited supply of en-

This is a vertical axis wind turbine (VAWT).

radioactive wastes. The radiation can hurt living cells. Also, the wastes produced in a nuclear power plant can stay radioactive for thousands of years. These wastes could pollute the earth's environment.

Tidal energy is being used in some parts of the world to produce energy. A large plant has recently been built in the Soviet Union. Tidal energy comes from the movement of the tides. To produce tidal energy, small dams are built across bays or tidal estuaries. An estuary is a low-lying area near the mouth of a river which flows into the ocean. The tide flows in and out of the estuary. The rising tide flows through an open gate in the dam. When the tide flows out, the water is trapped behind the dam. The water is then released to flow through generators. The generators produce electricity.

Wind energy has been used for hundreds of years. People in the Netherlands have been using windmills for many years to

ergy. In a nuclear plant, uranium atoms are split to make heat. The heat boils water to produce steam, which drives generators to make electricity. Many people have become concerned about the use of nuclear energy. Nuclear energy produces radiation and

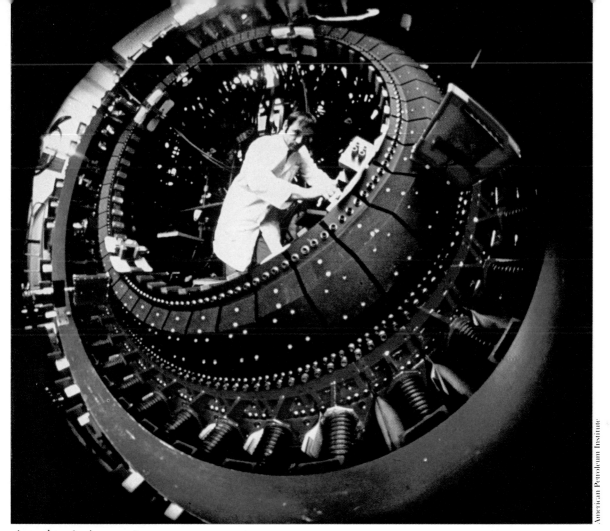

A nuclear fusion reactor.

grind grains and pump water. Some scientists have suggested that large windmills could be built in the U.S. to convert the wind's energy into electricity. A large experimental windmill has been built near Boone, North Carolina.

Unfortunately, wind power cannot be depended upon. Many times the wind may not blow. Also, the power generated by the windmill cannot be stored. Wind power will probably be a minor source of energy in the future.

Many scientists believe that the

heat found inside the earth could be a source of energy. The use of this underground heat is called geothermal energy. Geothermal energy can be tapped by drilling wells into underground sources of hot water and steam. The heat and steam produced by hot springs and geysers could be used to run electric-generating plants. Buildings could also be heated using geothermal energy. The harnessing of the energy from the earth's interior promises to be an important energy source of the future.

The future of people living on earth depends on energy. New areas which contain fossil fuels need to be found. Research must go on to find new ways to produce energy from coal, tar sands, and oil shales. New energy sources need to be developed. Most importantly, people must learn how to conserve energy. In this way, we will all have enough energy in the future.

A geothermal well.

American Petroleum In

PRONUNCIATION GUIDE

These symbols have the same sound as the darker letters in the sample words.

ə	balloon, ago
a	map, have
ä	father, car
b	ball, rib
d	did, add
e	bell, get
ē	keen, leap
f	fan, soft
g	good, big
h	hurt, ahead
i	rip, ill
ī	side, sky
j	join, germ
k	king, ask
l	let, cool
m	man, same
n	no, turn
ō	cone, know
ȯ	all, saw
p	part, scrap
r	root, tire
s	so, press
sh	shoot, machine
t	to, stand
ü	pool, lose
u̇	put, book
v	view, give
w	wood, glowing
y	yes, year
′	accent

GLOSSARY

These words are defined the way they are used in the text.

anthracite (an′ thrə sīt) a very hard, dark coal

bituminous (bə tü′ mə nəs) a soft coal that is easy to burn

coke (kōk) a material left over after coal is baked in special ovens

conservation (kän sər vā′ shən) the careful saving of energy and resources

derrick (der′ ik) a tower that holds machinery over a deep drill hole

gasification (gas ə fə kā′ shən) to change something into gas

generator (jen′ ə rāt ər) a machine that changes mechanical energy, such as a spinning wheel, into electrical energy

geologist (jē äl′ ə jəst) a person who studies the history of the earth and its rocks

gravimeter (gra vim′ ət ər) a machine that measures the pull of gravity

hydrocarbon (hī drə kär′ bən) a chemical made up of hydrogen and carbon

impermeable (im pər′ mē ə bəl) not allowing anything to pass through

lignite (lig′ nīt) a very soft, early kind of coal

magnetometer (mag nə täm′ ət ər) a machine that measure magnetic pull

47

pollution (pə lü′ shən) something that makes the air, earth or water dirty

refine (ri fīn′) to make something pure; places that clean and refine oil and gas are called refineries

sediment (sed′ə mənt) stones, mud, and gravel that harden to form sedimentary rock

seismograph (sīz′ mə graf) a machine that measures and records movement in the earth

shale (shāl) a kind of rock that can hold oil

INDEX